Maths Around Us

Shapes in the Kitchen

Tracey Steffora

Raintree

www.raintreepublishers.co.uk
Visit our website to find out
more information about
Raintree books.

To order:
☎ Phone 0845 6044371
📄 Fax +44 (0) 1865 312263
✉ Email myorders@raintreepublishers.co.uk

Customers from outside the UK please telephone +44 1865 312262

Raintree is an imprint of Capstone Global Library Limited,
a company incorporated in England and Wales having its
registered office at 7 Pilgrim Street, London, EC4V 6LB
– Registered company number: 6695582

Edited by Rebecca Rissman, Tracey Steffora, and Catherine Veitch
Designed by Joanna Hinton-Malivoire
Picture research by Elizabeth Alexander
Production by Victoria Fitzgerald
Originated by Capstone Global Library Ltd
Printed and bound in China by Leo Paper Products Ltd

ISBN 978 1 406 22315 6
15 14 13 12 11
10 9 8 7 6 5 4 3 2 1

British Library Cataloguing in Publication Data
Steffora, Tracey.
Shapes in the kitchen. -- (Maths around us)
516.1'5-dc22

Acknowledgements
The author and publisher are grateful to the following for
permission to reproduce photographs: Alamy pp. 7
(© Clearviewstock), 11 (© Palabra), 22 (© Directphoto.org), 23
glossary – tile (© Clearviewstock); GAP Interiors p. 5 (Spike
Powell); Getty Images pp. 4 (Travel Ink/Gallo Images), 12
(B. Sporrer/ J.Skowronek/ StockFood Creative); iStockphoto p. 20
(© Ljiljana Pavkov); Photolibrary p. 19 (Lynx/Iconotec.com);
Shutterstock pp. 8 (© Michael C. Gray), 9 (© David Hughes), 13
(© oku), 15 (© AnnalA), 16 (© Argunova), 17 (© VolkOFF-ZS-BP),
20 background (© Blackbirds), 21 (© highviews), 23 glossary
- cutting board (© VolkOFF-ZS-BP), 23 glossary – samosa
(© highviews).

Cover photograph of a meal viewed from above reproduced with
permission of Getty Images (Andy Crawford/Dorling Kindersley),
wood pattern reproduced with permission of Shutterstock
(© Blackbirds). Back cover photograph of a napkin reproduced
with permission of iStockphoto (© Ljiljana Pavkov), wood pattern
reproduced with permission of Shutterstock (© Blackbirds).

We would like to thank Nancy Harris, Dee Reid, and Diana Bentley
for their assistance in the preparation of this book.

Every effort has been made to contact copyright holders of
material reproduced in this book. Any omissions will be rectified in
subsequent printings if notice is given to the publisher.

Contents

Shapes around us

Shapes are everywhere.

There are many shapes in the
kitchen.

Squares

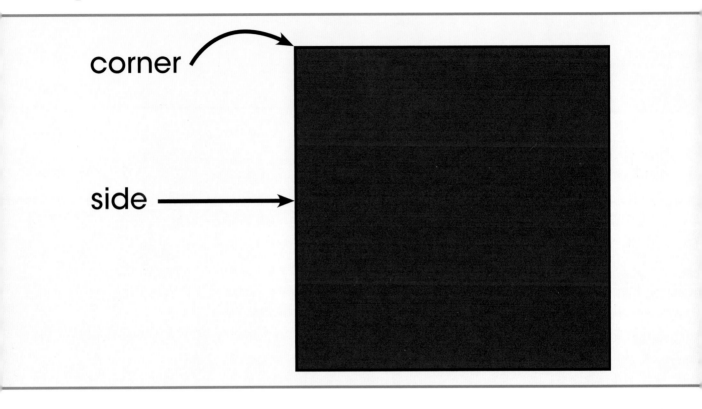

corner

side

A square has four sides.

A square has four corners.

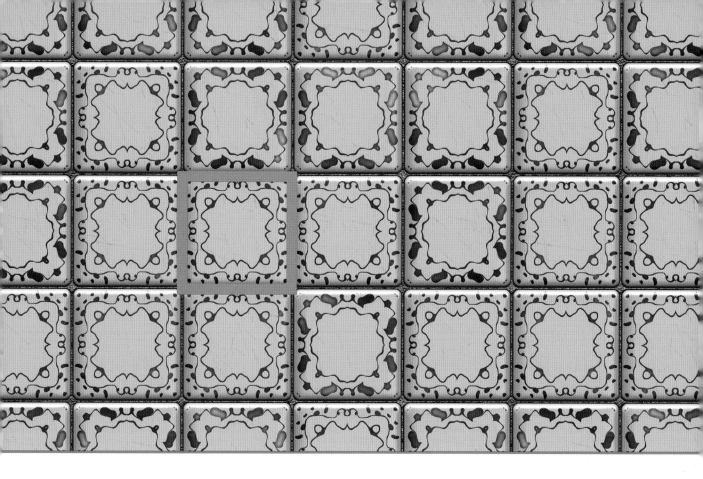

This tile is a square.

This cheese is a square.

This window is a square.

Circles

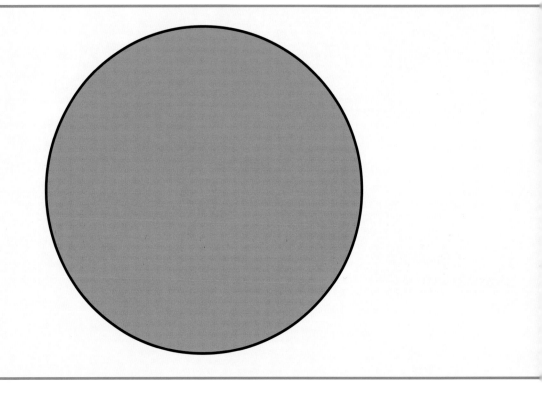

A circle is a round shape.

It has no corners.

This plughole is a circle.

This apple is a circle.

This plate is a circle.

Rectangles

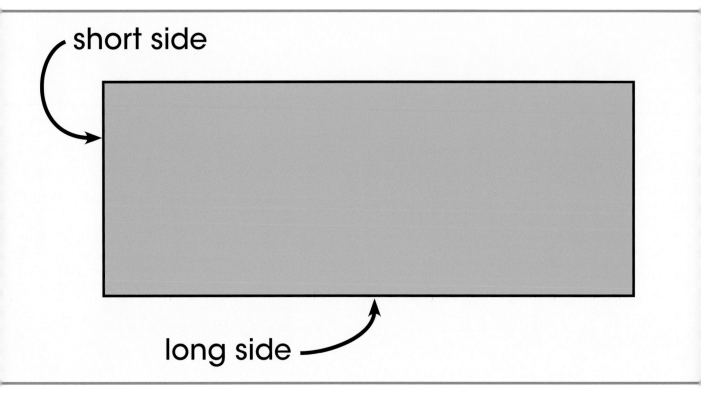

short side

long side

A rectangle has four sides.

A rectangle has four corners.

This door is a rectangle.

This sponge is a rectangle.

This chopping board is a rectangle.

Triangles

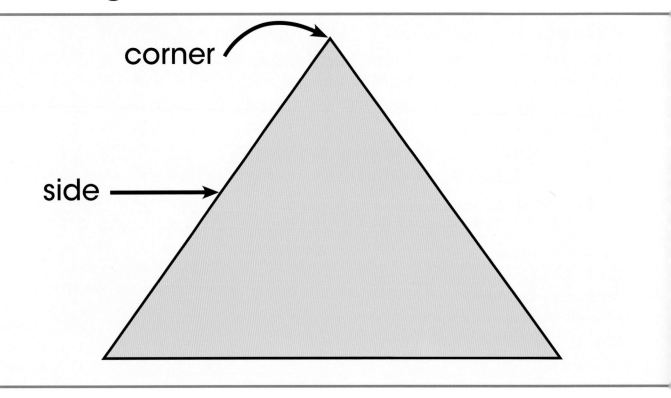

A triangle has three sides.

A triangle has three corners.

This sandwich is a triangle.

This napkin is a triangle.

This samosa is a triangle.

Shapes in the kitchen

How many shapes can you see?

Picture glossary

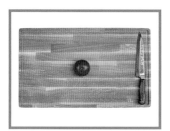

chopping board board used for cutting or chopping food

samosa pastry filled with meat or vegetables. It is shaped in a triangle.

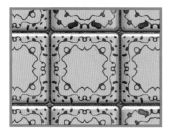

tile piece of material used to cover floors or walls

Index

Notes for parents and teachers

Before reading

Review the basic shapes circle, square, rectangle, and triangle with children. Have children name things in their environment that demonstrate each of the shapes. You might also show them that if you cut a potato in half, you will have a curvilinear shape that can be dipped in ink or paint to make a round or oval stamp (depending on which way you slice it).

After reading

- Have children pay attention to shapes during lunch and report back which shapes they found in their food or food containers.
- Extend by reviewing or introducing children to other shapes, such as oval, ellipse, rhombus, diamond, or hexagon. Discuss the characteristics of these shapes and have children identify them in their environment.